Whales and Dolphins

CONTENTS

© Aladdin Books Ltd

Designed and produced by
Aladdin Books Ltd
70 Old Compton Street
London W1

All rights reserved

Printed in Belgium

First published in the
United States in 1985 by
Gloucester Press
387 Park Avenue South
New York NY 10016

ISBN 0-531-17015-2

Library of Congress
Catalog Card No. 85-80643

Certain illustrations have previously appeared in the "Civilization Library"
series published by Gloucester Press.

Whales and Dolphins

ELIZABETH STRACHAN

Illustrated by
NORMAN WEAVER

Consultant
JOYCE POPE

Gloucester Press
New York · Toronto · 1985

Giants of the deep

The word "whale" brings to mind a picture of a huge creature. This is hardly surprising since some whales are very large indeed. The Blue whale, which averages 25m (82ft) in length, is the largest creature the world has ever known – larger even than the prehistoric Brontosaurus. But there are nearly 100 species of whale, and many are much smaller. Their close cousins – the dolphins and porpoises – are usually less than 4m (13ft) long.

Sea-dwelling mammals

Whales are mammals that spend their entire life cycles in the water. While most mammals can swim, very few live in water for the whole of their lives. Whales, dolphins and porpoises do: they feed and give birth in the sea.

These sea-dwellers are the descendants of a four-legged animal that once lived on land. It took to living in the water to find food and escape from its enemies. As its descendants adapted to life in the sea, they gradually came to resemble fish.

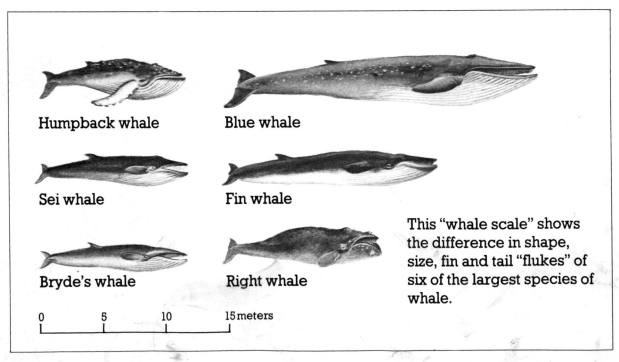

Humpback whale

Blue whale

Sei whale

Fin whale

Bryde's whale

Right whale

This "whale scale" shows the difference in shape, size, fin and tail "flukes" of six of the largest species of whale.

0   5   10   15 meters

A Humpback whale leaps
clear of the ocean,
displaying its huge flippers
and grooved throat.
Humpbacks are among the
ocean giants, and have
distinctive bumps and
knobs on the head and
flippers.

An essential difference

Because whales spend the whole of their lives in the water they might easily be thought to be fish. But they are very different. Like all mammals they are warm-blooded, and have a thick layer of fat, or "blubber," under their skin that protects them from the cold. While fish are covered in scales, whales have smooth, delicate skin. Fish fins are supported by bone, while a whale's back or "dorsal" fin is solid and muscular.

How whales swim

Whales have the ability to move the ends of their bodies up and down – the action that galloping land mammals use. They make this movement when they swim, and also use their tail flukes to push against the water and so move themselves along.

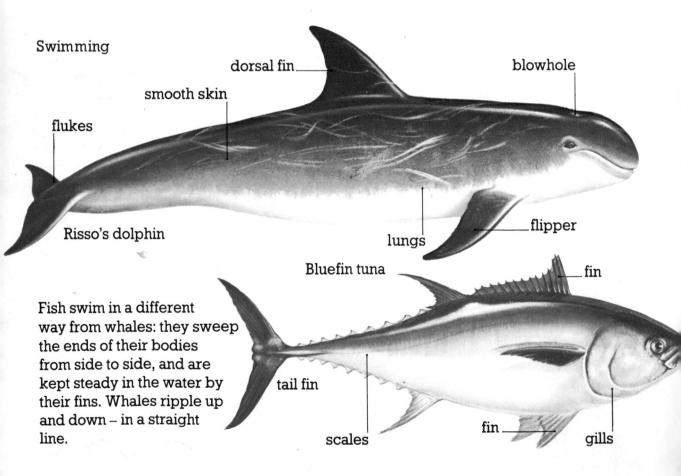

Swimming

dorsal fin

blowhole

smooth skin

flukes

Risso's dolphin

lungs

flipper

Bluefin tuna

fin

Fish swim in a different way from whales: they sweep the ends of their bodies from side to side, and are kept steady in the water by their fins. Whales ripple up and down – in a straight line.

tail fin

scales

fin

gills

How whales breathe

All mammals need to breathe air to survive, and whales are specially adapted to do this. They have lungs and take in air through nostrils, formed from a single, or double, "blowhole" on top of the head. While they can hold their breath for a time — up to an hour in some cases — they have to surface regularly to "blow." They pant deeply and a column of vapor rises above them, formed when the warm air from their lungs meets the air outside.

Family and friends

Whales live in groups which often number only three or four. They take care of each other and have been seen to help sick or injured comrades by holding them up in the water to prevent drowning.

Calves stay close to their mothers' sides for up to a year. Sometimes other females, who have not yet borne calves, act as "nursemaids" and help to look after the young.

Sensory systems

The sense organs of whales are highly adapted to life in the water. The eyesight of whales is not sharp, but they can see in shallow water and in open air. They have a very well-developed sense of hearing, and have evolved a system of "echo-location." They send out sounds through their blowholes and judge – from the returning echoes – the distance of the object or prey.

Whale songs

Whales are sociable creatures and keep in touch with each other by making many different noises – including squeaks, whistles and clicks, thumps, knocks and low-pitched moans. Sounds travel well in water – the musical moaning of the Humpback can be heard up to 200km (124 miles) away.

Whalers in the nineteenth century called these sounds "whale songs." They were able to pick out the voices of different whales including the Humpback, the Right, the Gray and the Bowhead. We now have much more information about the sounds particular whales make: for example, short clicks are made by Grays and Blues.

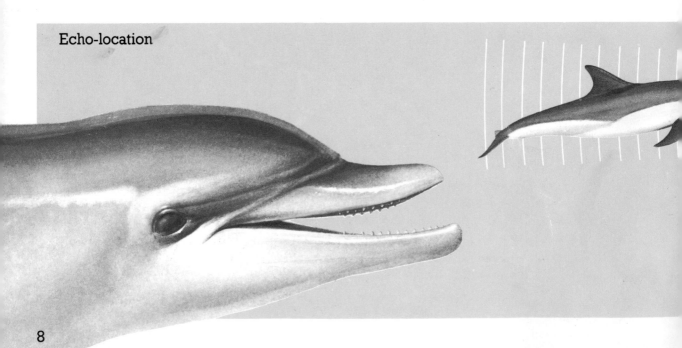

Echo-location

This tame Killer whale leaps for a fish in a dolphinarium. Because it is above water, it uses its eyesight to judge the distance of the food offered.

A whale (or dolphin), nearing an object underwater bombards it with bleeps of high-pitched sound. The echoes from these bleeps bounce back to the whale's ears, which are located deep in its skull. The whale can then work out the distance and speed of the obstruction or prey.

Migration and reproduction

Whales can live in warm or cold water. Many species migrate constantly between the polar waters where they feed and the warmer waters where the calves are born. However, few whales ever cross the Equator.

Birth

Whales mate like other mammals, and the females give birth between nine months and a year later. Baby whales – like the Humpback in the picture – have to be able to swim as soon as they are born, so they are large and well-developed at birth: in the case of the Humpback, 4.5m (14.5ft) long, nearly a third of the size of its mother.

As soon as the calf is born another whale may push it up to the surface to take its first breath of air. The calf feeds on its mother's rich, fatty milk and by the end of its first year will measure 8m (26ft).

Humpback whales

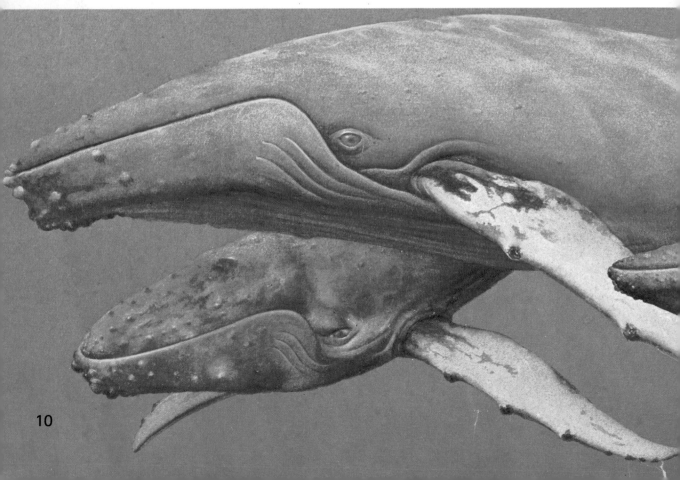

Between December and March each year, hundreds of Gray whales swim south, down the west coast of North America. They are migrating from their Arctic feeding grounds to the warmer waters off Mexico, where the females give birth. A few days after the calves are born the whales swim back to the cold waters. They summer in the Arctic, and feed on the rich supplies of shrimp-like "krill" now available.

Barrow

Vancouver

Pacific Ocean

San Francisco

San Diego

Gray whale

11

The baleens

A baleen whale has no teeth. Instead, long, frayed sheets of finely meshed whalebone hang down from the roof of its mouth. The Blue whale has an average of 324 of these "baleen" plates on each jaw; each is triangular and may be more than 1.6m (3.5ft) wide. Baleen whales feed upon shoals of krill, trapping the shrimps in the baleen as they draw water into their mouths.

The baleen families

The three main family groups of baleens are the slow Right whales, the Gray whales and the streamlined Rorquals. No one can give an explanation for their great size, but it could be that the ease with which they gather their food, and the buoyancy of the water, has put no restriction on their growth.

Right whale

How baleens trap their food

The inner edge of each baleen plate is frayed and whiskery so the long legs and antennae of the tiny prey are easily snagged in it. The problem that baleen whales have is how to get large quantities of water past their baleen plates, and strain out the food, without swallowing the water. This is why baleens have been seen swimming slowly through great shoals of krill and then surfacing and rolling from side to side; this action makes the water pour out of their mouths, leaving the shrimps entangled in their baleen plates.

Gulpers and skimmers

Within the baleen families there are two more distinctions. The "gulpers" (Blue, Fin, Piked and Humpback) take great gulps of water and squeeze it out from the sides of their mouths. The "skimmers" (Great Right and Bowhead) simply catch their food by swimming along with their mouths open.

baleen

Fin whale

Human

Right and Gray whales

Right whales were given their name because, in the early days of whaling, they were the "right" whales to hunt. They were an easier target than others, for the early whalers with their open boats and simple harpoons, because they were slow-moving and gentle and did not sink when killed. They also have the longest baleen plates and so were valued for their whalebone, which was used as support for undergarments. They were hunted almost to extinction, and few now survive.

Types of Right whales

The Bowhead, which lives in the Arctic and is now very rare, is still hunted by the Inuit (Eskimos). It is the only whale to remain in cold waters to breed. Both the Bowhead and its cousin, the Great Right whale (pictured below), are large – they average 15m (49ft). At 5m (16.5ft) the Pygmy Right is the smallest of the baleens.

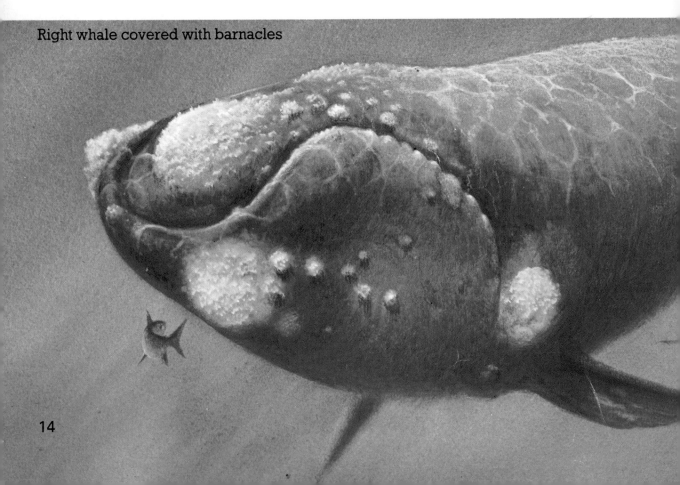

Right whale covered with barnacles

Friendly Grays

The Gray whale is a single species. Unlike the Right whales and the Rorquals it does not have a dorsal fin, but it does have two short throat grooves. It is also hairy, with bristles on the top of its head and along the lower jaw, and tufts on its snout. It is about 12.2m (40ft) long.

The Gray whale was an easy target for the early whalers, because it comes close inshore to give birth and to feed. It is now a protected species and its annual migration, from the Arctic to the warmer breeding grounds off the west coast of North America, is a big tourist attraction. Grays seem to enjoy attention, and individuals have even come up to boats to have their snouts patted!

Like all animals, whales have their own particular parasites. These include large barnacles, known only from the whales on which they live, and skin lice (above) which make hard patches form on the whale's skin.

Rorquals

Most baleen whales are Rorquals, a name which comes from the Norwegian word meaning "pleated." Rorquals have a deeply grooved throat area that can expand, allowing them to take in great gulps of water as they feed. They have a small dorsal fin set well down the back near the tail. This appears above the water as the whale begins to dive or "sound."

Fast Fins

There are six species of Rorquals, ranging in size from the Blue whale, which may top 30m (98.5ft), to the Minke whale, which averages 8m (26ft). The Fin whale is next in size to the Blue and it is also the fastest, able to swim at more than 20 knots an hour. All Rorquals are streamlined, fast-moving animals. In the past this made them difficult to catch, but today they are no match for the spotter aircraft and powerful ships of the whaling industry.

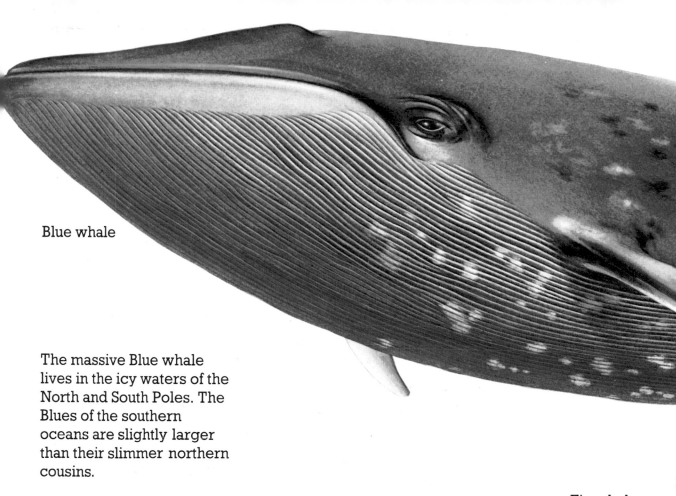

Blue whale

The massive Blue whale
lives in the icy waters of the
North and South Poles. The
Blues of the southern
oceans are slightly larger
than their slimmer northern
cousins.

Fin whales

Toothed whales

All whales, dolphins and porpoises which have teeth – rather than baleen plates – are put into this category. There are many species of toothed whales, with a great variety of shapes and sizes. The Sperm whale is one of the giants while the Common porpoise is only about 1.4m (4.5ft) long. Some may have as many as 200 teeth in their jaws while others – in spite of their name – have none! Toothed whales eat fish and squid (a relative of the octopus).

Color, patterns and fins

Toothed whales range in color from black through to gray and white. The Sperm whale is usually a dark steely gray, but it lightens with age and older males can turn white – like the legendary Moby Dick. Some toothed whales do not have a dorsal fin while the Killer whale's is tall and pointed.

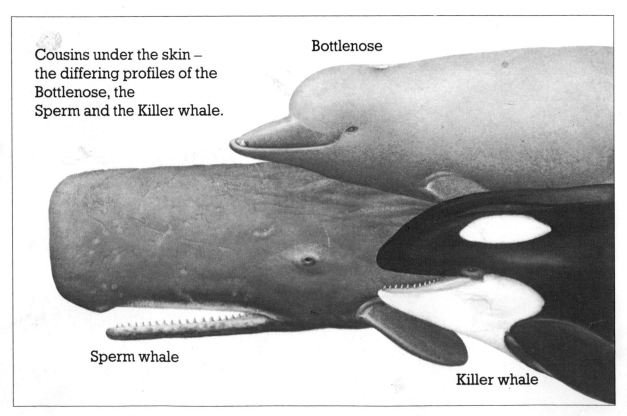

Cousins under the skin – the differing profiles of the Bottlenose, the Sperm and the Killer whale.

Bottlenose

Sperm whale

Killer whale

Sperm whales

The huge head of the Sperm whale contains about one ton of an oil called "spermaceti," and overhangs the tooth-filled lower jaw. The rare Pygmy is a small relation.

Beaked and Bottlenose

These whales are found in all the world's oceans, living in the deepest waters. They are shy of ships, and so little is known about their behavior.

Narwhals and Belugas

Male Narwhals have an ivory tooth which grows forward from the left upper jaw. Narwhals and Belugas live in polar waters.

Dolphins

Most toothed whales are dolphins. Common and Bottlenose are the best-known. Many have long snouts; a few short-nosed types are generally called porpoises.

River dolphins

This group includes some very rare species which live in the murky waters of large tropical rivers. They all have long snouts and tiny eyes.

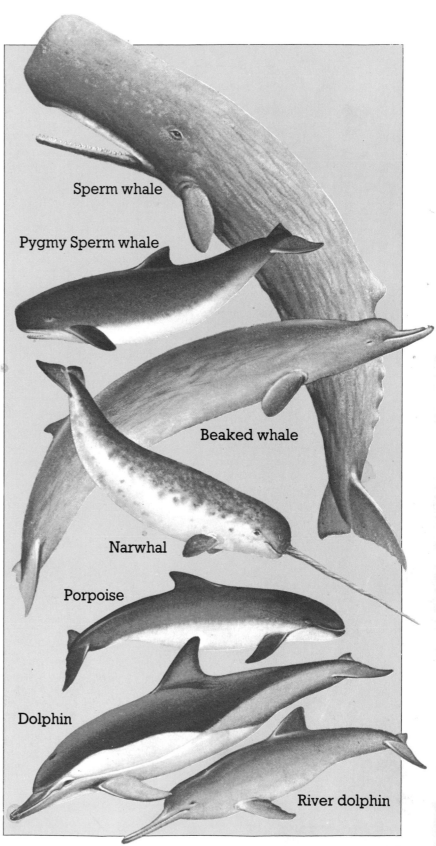

Sperm whale

Pygmy Sperm whale

Beaked whale

Narwhal

Porpoise

Dolphin

River dolphin

The Sperm whale

At 15m (49ft) the Sperm whale is the largest of all the toothed whales. The sight of its strange square head, overhanging its tooth-filled, gaping lower jaw must have been a terrifying sight to the early whalers as they approached it in their fragile boats. Sperm whales were a highly prized catch, hunted in particular for the valuable oil inside the head.

Sperm whales and squids

Sperm whales feed on large fish and squids. They may stun these with a stream of high-pitched sound, disabling the prey so that it can then be swallowed. The only certain knowledge that we have of some deep sea fish and squid comes from examining the contents of the stomachs of Sperm whales.

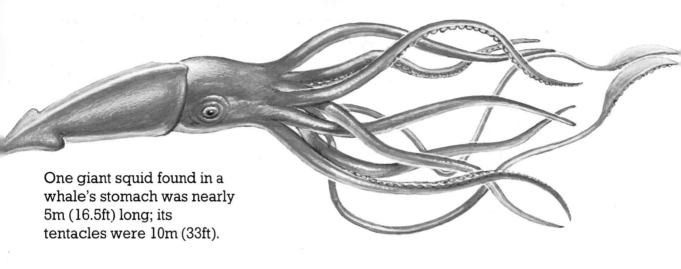

One giant squid found in a whale's stomach was nearly 5m (16.5ft) long; its tentacles were 10m (33ft).

Deep divers

Sperm whales are the deepest divers of all whales, and can reach depths of 1,000m (3,280ft) to find their prey. A Sperm whale's teeth are located in its narrow lower jaws only. We do not really know how they work. Those of a young whale are sharp and pointed, but as the animal ages they are worn flat.

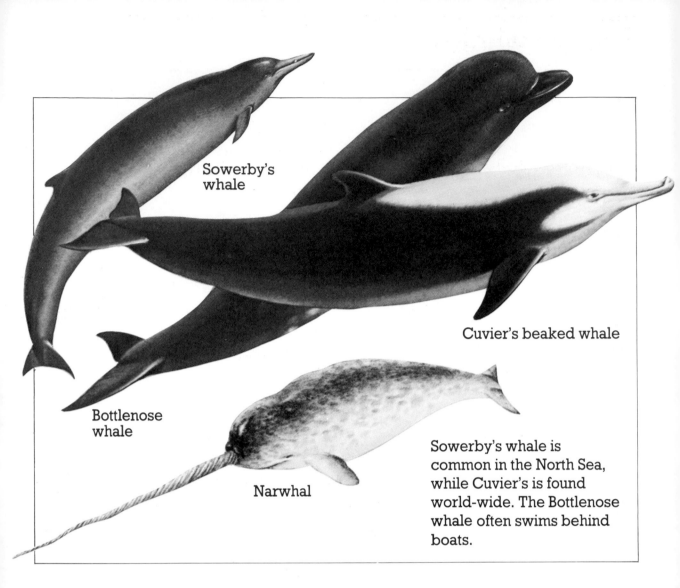

Sowerby's whale

Cuvier's beaked whale

Bottlenose whale

Narwhal

Sowerby's whale is common in the North Sea, while Cuvier's is found world-wide. The Bottlenose whale often swims behind boats.

Beluga young often swim in single file behind their mother. They travel through narrow lanes in the pack ice, where they may fall prey to Inuit (Eskimo) hunters.

Smaller whales

Several species of small and medium-sized whales are known. Up to 10m (33ft) long, they include the Beaked whales – which are seen only very occasionally – and the Bottlenose whale, which is known to have held its breath for over an hour – a record among whales!

Narwhals and Belugas

These are whales of the icy waters of the Arctic. The blotchy-gray Narwhal is well-known. It has also been called the Unicorn whale because the males have a single long tooth which grows out through a hole in the upper lip to form a spiral tusk. Very rarely, females may also have one, or two, shorter tusks.

"Sea canaries"

Beluga calves are liver-colored at birth. By the age of six they have lightened in color, becoming a creamy white all over. Belugas are famous for the sounds they make as they travel among the ice floes. Sailors used to call them "sea canaries" because of the birdlike, whistling noises they make which reveal their presence.

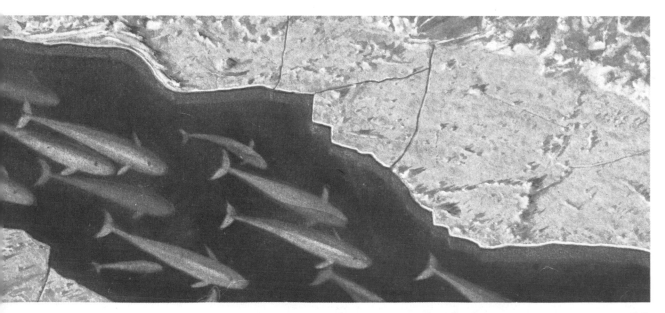

Killers!

Killer whales, which average 8m (26ft) in length, are members of the dolphin family. They are found mainly in the cold polar seas of the northern and southern oceans. Their blunt jaws contain about 40 sharply pointed teeth, with which they attack a wide variety of prey. But humans are apparently safe.

A giant baleen whale is no match for a pack of Killers. They can outswim and outmaneuver the larger animal, biting it until it is exhausted.

The food of Killer whales

Killers are the only whales to feed on mammals, and these even include other whales and dolphins. They hunt in packs which may number 30 or 40 and no penguin or seal is safe from them. They even attack large baleen whales, tearing at the tongue and throat until the ocean giant is crippled and finally killed.

The Killers' back fin

Killers have thick-set bodies, and are black with a white belly. They also have a white spot above and behind the eye. But the feature by which they are most easily recognized is the sharp, black fin which rises as they cruise just below the surface of the water. An old male's fin may be as high as 2m (6.5ft).

Killers also use their fins to judge their position beneath the ice. They are noted for their skill and cunning at working among ice floes. If a penguin or seal is taking refuge on a floe, Killers will rush up and heave the floe with their heads, breaking or tilting the ice and sending the animal toppling into the water.

Penguins fall prey to this Killer. By balancing on their tails (below) Killers peer onto the ice, to see if any animal is taking refuge there.

Dolphins and porpoises

Common dolphin

Bottlenose dolphin

White-sided dolphin

Commerson's dolphin

Hourglass dolphin

The commonest whales are those between 2m and 4m (6.5ft and 13ft) in length. In general, if they have pointed or "beaked" faces they are dolphins; if they have short faces they are porpoises. Large groups, or "schools," of more than a thousand animals are sometimes seen.

"Porpoising"

Dolphins and porpoises often travel in a way known as "porpoising." The animals swim through the surface waters of the sea, diving and then surging up, sometimes leaping clear of the water. As their heads break the surface, they open their nostrils and take a breath of air.

Dolphins are very acrobatic and sometimes, as they leap, they spin in the air. They also seem to enjoy riding in the waves behind boats; with a swimming speed of up to 30 knots, they can outpace many vessels.

Pilot whales frequently become stranded in shallow water. Once one is in distress, others try to help it and then become beached themselves.

Stranded whales

Dolphins, porpoises and occasionally larger whales can often be seen in inshore waters. They are safe where the water is deep, but sometimes they become stranded on a shelving beach — perhaps because their echo-location system does not give them any information about the decreasing depth of the water. Once ashore they are helpless, for their streamlined shape cannot be properly supported in the air. Even when humans try to help, the animals often die.

Dolphins are popular
performers and seem to
like their human captors.
The owners of aquariums
have learned not to put
dolphins and sharks in the
same pool, for the dolphins
will usually kill the sharks.

A special relationship

People have been especially aware of dolphins since early times, and there are many stories about them, some of which date back to the ancient Greeks. In most of these accounts the dolphins feature as friendly creatures, helpful to human beings. There are even reports of people in difficulty in the sea being helped by dolphins, who seem to treat the human as a distressed member of their own kind.

But in other respects, dolphins are not well-liked. They eat fish, and fishermen sometimes kill them. Some countries would like to continue whaling by hunting dolphins, but fortunately this is not yet widespread.

Dolphins in captivity

In recent years, dolphins – including Killers – and small whales have been kept successfully in large aquariums. Often their lifespan in captivity is short, but they have sometimes settled happily enough to breed.

Because of their intelligence dolphins have been used – experimentally at least – to help in underwater construction work, carrying tools and performing simple tasks.

Whale future

The ruthless whaling of the nineteenth century and the first half of the twentieth drastically reduced the numbers of the great whales. The invention of the explosive harpoon and the introduction of fleets of factory ships meant that whales were slaughtered by the thousand. In the Antarctic, between 1930 and 1931, 30,000 Blue whales were killed in one season. Since then, bodies such as the International Whaling Commission have been set up, to study whale populations and set limits on catches.

The massive tail flukes of a Sperm whale about to dive. While this species is now fully protected in some oceans, it is still hunted in others.

Saving the whales

With greater controls on the whaling industry, the number of whales is very slowly recovering. But some species are still under threat – for example, there are probably fewer than 10,000 Blue whales worldwide. In the long run, the only way to protect whales is to avoid buying goods that contain whale products. There should be no need for the further destruction of these fascinating, and still largely unknown, sea-dwelling mammals.

Glossary

Baleen Fringed sheets of whalebone which hang down from the upper jaws of baleen whales. These whales do not have teeth.

Blubber The layers of fat on a whale's body.

Blowhole A whale's nostrils. The blowhole is situated on top of the whale's head, and a flap of skin keeps water out when the whale dives below the sea.

Dolphinarium An aquarium which specializes in keeping whales and dolphins, where the public can observe them.

Echo-location The means by which whales and dolphins judge the distance and shapes of objects, using sounds and their returning echoes.

Mammals Warm-blooded animals which have milk glands and "breast-feed" their young. They may have skin, hair or fur on their bodies.

Migration The seasonal movement of animals or birds from one climatic temperature zone to another; in the case of the Gray whales, from polar waters to warmer waters.

Spermaceti The clear, waxy oil found in the head of the Sperm whale.

Index

PRINTED IN BELGIUM BY

proost
INTERNATIONAL BOOK PRODUCTION